HELEN
KELLER

KATHERINE RAWSON

TABLE OF CONTENTS

In 1880, the Keller family
lived on a farm in Alabama.
June 27 was a happy
day for them. On that day,
their first daughter,
Helen, was born.
Helen was a healthy baby.
At the age of six months,
she began to talk.
She could say "tea"
and "wah wah" (water).

➤ "Ivy Green," the birthplace of Helen Keller
in Tuscumbia, Ala.

At one year old,

Helen began to walk.

She loved to explore

the world around her.

She was happy in her family's

pretty, white house.

Then, in 1882,

a terrible thing happened.

Helen became sick

with a bad fever

and almost died.

Her parents were very worried.

After a few days,

Helen began to get better.

The fever went away,

but there was still something wrong.

When Helen's mother

waved her hand

in front of Helen's eyes,

Helen didn't see it.

When the dinner bell rang,

Helen didn't hear it.

The fever had made Helen

blind and deaf.

She was only 19 months old.

Now Helen lived

in a silent, dark world.

All day, she held

onto her mother's skirt

and followed her

around the house.

She couldn't see anything,

so she touched everything.

That was how she learned

about the world around her.

Since Helen couldn't hear,
she didn't learn to talk.
Instead, she used motions
to communicate.
She pulled on someone
to mean "come."
She pushed to mean "go."
She rubbed her hand on her face
when she wanted her mother.
She sucked her thumb
to mean her baby sister, Mildred.

Helen couldn't talk, but she did laugh when she was happy. She also screamed when she was angry. Helen was often angry. It was very hard to live in a dark and silent world.

➤ A young Helen Keller sits with her dog.

Helen knew that other people talked.
Sometimes, she touched their lips
when they talked.

She moved her lips in the same way,
but she still couldn't talk.

This made her very frustrated,
and she screamed even more.

Helen would not sit quietly
at the dinner table. Instead,
she ran around and took food
from other people's plates.
Her parents didn't know
how to help her.

Helen also couldn't read or write.
One day, Helen's father talked
with some people
at a special school.

The school was called
the Perkins School for the Blind.
They said they could help Helen.
They sent a teacher
to live with Helen and her family.
That teacher's name
was Anne Sullivan.

Helen with her teacher Anne Sullivan in 1893.

In March 1887, when Helen was almost seven years old, Anne arrived

at the Keller house.

She had a present

for Helen. It was a doll.

Helen hugged the doll close.

Then Anne took Helen's hand and used her fingers to spell "doll," *d-o-l-l.*

Some deaf people use finger spelling
as a way of communicating.
Anne tried to teach
finger spelling to Helen.
She spelled *d-o-l-l* in Helen's hand.
Helen copied her.
She learned to spell "doll"
and many other words.
She thought it was a fun game,
but she didn't understand
that this was a way
she could communicate.

One day, Anne and Helen
went to get water from the pump.
Helen put her hand
under the cold water.
Anne spelled "water," *w-a-t-e-r*,
with Helen's other hand.
Suddenly, Helen understood.
W-a-t-e-r meant the cold thing
on her hand. Now Helen knew
that everything had a name.

➤ At this pump, behind her birthplace in Tuscumbia, AL, Helen Keller learned to spell the word "water".

Helen was very excited. She wanted
to learn the names of everything.
On that first day, she learned
30 new words. The most important
word was "teacher."
Teacher became the name
that Helen always called Anne.

Finger spelling gave Helen

a way to communicate

with other people.

Now Anne could teach

her many things.

Anne taught Helen how

to read and write.

First, she used special paper

that had raised letters.

Later, Helen learned

to read Braille, a system

of letters made for blind people

The letters in Braille are made

with raised dots.

Anne opened up the world for Helen. Now Helen could talk with other people. She could read and write. She wasn't angry anymore.

Young Helen Keller sits with a book at her desk.

Helen kept on learning.

When she was a young woman,

she went to college.

Anne Sullivan sat next to her

in all of her classes.

Helen worked hard

her whole life to help

other people, especially blind

and deaf people.

She traveled around the world,

and met many famous people.

She had many friends.

Helen died in 1968,
at the age of 88.
She had lived a long
and meaningful life.

In cap and gown, Helen Keller is shown as she graduated cum laude from Radcliffe College.

1880 Born June 27 in Alabama

1882 After a severe illness, Helen is blind and deaf

1887 Anne Sullivan arrives to teach Helen

1900 Goes to Radcliffe College

1904 Graduates from college and publishes her first book

1936 Former teacher and companion, Anne Sullivan, dies

1968 Helen dies at age 88